Solo Full-time RVing On A Budget

Go Small, Go Now

Becky Schade

Table of Contents

Part 1: Introduction   **4**
1A: Don't wait, go RVing now   4
1B: Who are you to be telling me how to do this?   5
1C: How this guide is organized   6
Part 2: RV Selection   **7**
2A: Go small, live big   7
2B: Picking your perfect small RV   9
2C: Taking the scary out of used RVs   11
2D: Dry weight, CCC, and GVWR?   13
2E: Demystifying tow vehicles   15
Part 3: Money   **17**
3A: How to calculate how much money you need to go   17
full-timing
3B: Avoiding debt   20
3C: Option 1: Delaying departure to save up more money   21
3D: Option 2: Take what you have for money and go now   23
3E: RVing costs once on the road compared to living   24
stationary
3F: Earning a living on the road   27
Part 4: Small RVing Answers   **32**
4A: How to organize and make the most of your limited   32
space in a small RV
4B: Cooking in a small RV   33
4C: Small RV, cold weather   35
4D: Pets in a Small RV   39
Part 5: Solo RVing Answers   **42**
5A: Solo RVer safety   42
5B: Loneliness   44
5C: Having to do it all yourself   49
Part 6: Wrapping Up   **52**
Appendix   **53**
The Perfect Small RV Worksheet   53
The RV Inspection and Question Checklist   58
The Perfect Tow Vehicle Worksheet   62
The Money Worksheet   64
Further Study   67

Part 1
Introduction

1A: Don't wait, go RVing now

Our society's rules about life as an adult are unwritten, but still very real: work comes before play. Spend the first 40+ years of adulthood working as hard as you can, in order to spend the last 15-20 enjoying the Good Life.

Back during the Industrial Revolution this mindset allowed America to make great progress and afforded the working class a prosperous retirement, but times have changed and this model's heyday is long gone. Retirement is no longer as certain as it used to be. The days of sticking with one company for decades in return for a generous retirement package are past. More people are having to work into their later years past the traditional retirement age, the uncertain economic climate is playing havoc on investing and 401k plans, and who knows what state Social Security will be in ten, twenty, or thirty years from now.

Despite this, conventional wisdom still says the safest way make it through life unscathed is to follow the rules and hold a steady long-term job. I know 5.7 percent of the population who beg to differ, the current national unemployment rate. That's more than one in twenty people who are capable and willing to hold a job but are currently unable to find one. That doesn't sound safe, that sounds like a gamble.

Even if you play by the rules and win the career lottery, there are other obstacles that could keep you from your RVing dream in retirement. You might not be physically healthy enough to go RVing at that point, or family obligations could keep you from getting on the road.

A small but growing number of people are looking at the hazy future and deciding to take the plunge into full-time RVing before retirement instead.

This approach might earn you curious stares and doubting comments from your coworkers and relatives. It will take more effort than a 9 to 5 existence, and it will probably require more thinking and planning than you are used to doing. But the payoff is feeling truly alive, instead of just going through the motions. It's quieting that voice in the back of your mind that's been telling you there's something you're missing. It's waking up in the mornings with a smile thinking about the adventure ahead, instead of dreading the daily grind. It's living life to the fullest, right now, instead of in some uncertain future.

You've been dreaming about going full-time RVing. It's time to make that dream a reality.

"That sounds great, but..."

I can almost hear the chorus of 'buts' ringing back to me across time, along with all the reasons why you think the full-time RVing lifestyle won't work for you even though it sounds like exactly what you want to do.

The number one reason I hear is money. Only retired rich folks with great pensions go full-time RVing, right? Definitely not true. You'll need some money of course, but the second section of this guide is devoted to working out how it can be done on a limited budget by getting a small RV, and the third section goes into money details even further. No need to save up for years or sign your left arm away for a luxury motorcoach when for a much lower price you can get started much sooner. We'll also talk about how to handle some of the unique challenges that come from having a smaller rig.

"But I don't have anyone to go with!" I hear that quite a bit too, and it also shouldn't keep you from your dreams. Maybe you're worried about having to maintain everything on the RV by yourself. Maybe you're wondering about your personal safety. Or perhaps it's the question of loneliness. This guide will also address those concerns.

1B: Who are you to be telling me how to do this?

I've been teaching people about full-timing since November 2011 on my blog, Interstellar Orchard. In March of 2012 I purchased my small RV, and six weeks later it became my home. Then on September 14th of that year, I hit the road as a full-timer. I've been traveling and working my way around the country ever since, a young single woman who is not independently wealthy and who had no prior experience with RVs before buying mine. I've learned a lot of lessons in that time, and now I'm passing that knowledge on to you.

Full-time RVing when you're not rich can be a daunting prospect. It's hard to figure out where to start, and easy to worry about what could happen if you fail. While no two people's path to full-timing is going to look the same, I discovered when I was preparing to hit the road that I was able to take bits and pieces from several folks who were already on the road, and cobble that together with my own intuition to make a plan that worked for me. Armed with this kind of knowledge, the whole process became less scary.

It's easier to summon the courage to push past those scary "what-ifs" when you can read about how others have handled those "what-ifs" themselves. It's easier to muster the willpower to keep working hard on this dream that might not become reality for months or even years when you can read about others' success stories and see where that hard work paid off.

I am of the strong opinion that while a little determination, planning, and money are necessary to pursue a life on the road, equally helpful is the boost of confidence and knowledge gained from others who have been there before. That's where I come in.

1C: How this guide is organized

You'll quickly find that the steps to getting on the road are more fluid than a simple 1, 2, 3. This guide is split into several sections about specific parts of the RVing equation. Parts 2 and 3 are in roughly chronological order and have worksheets that go along with them (found in the appendix) that you will want to fill out as you go. Parts 4 and 5 deal with issues unique to small and solo RVing.

Feel free to skip the sections that don't apply to you and jump around to read what is. Take what's useful and craft your outline for freedom.

Part 2
RV Selection

2A: Go small, live big

When people think of full-time RVing, what usually comes to mind is one of those Class A bus-style motorcoaches that costs a couple hundred thousand dollars, or one of those three-axle 5th wheels that gets pulled behind a heavy duty or industrial sized truck. When that's the standard folks go by, of course full-timing seems inaccessible to all but the wealthiest people.

I had $23,500 in the bank when I started this adventure, and know people who had considerably less than that. Being smart with what money you do have and creative about the other resources at your disposal will take you far. My first big not-so-secret to getting on the road sooner rather than later is to go small; that is, get a small RV.

Obviously a smaller RV is going to require less savings up front to purchase, and get you on the road faster. But most people never look beyond that to the other benefits. They cost less money to maintain because there's, well, less of it to break. If by some extreme misfortune your small RV were to get totaled in an accident, it would cost less to replace. Small RVs are also going to have better gas mileage on average than larger ones, which saves even more money.

There are other benefits to a smaller RV besides the monetary ones. They're less stressful to drive in big cities or on crowded roadways because you need less room to pass and change lanes if, for instance, you find yourself in an exit only lane. And if the other drivers around you are being particularly rude and not letting you leave the exit lane (you'll have to excuse them, they're still stuck in the rat race you have escaped), it's also easier to find a turn around to accommodate your smaller size to get back up on the highway. Also:

- Many small RVs can fit into standard parking spots, which makes it

easier to get into attractions, fill up on gas, and go shopping.
- They require less time and effort to keep clean and organized.
- They're less likely to bottom out on uneven dirt roads, being shorter and with less space between the front and back wheels.

Now, a word or two on what is seen as the most obvious negative of small RVs–less room.

When people find out that I'm perfectly comfortable in 100 square feet of living space, I get a lot of skeptical looks.

Realize that as a full-timer you can choose to follow good weather year-round, and that means your living space includes your porch and back yard too, as well as all the neat parks, museums, beaches, historic sites, shops, restaurants, and everything else you'll visit on your travels. The trick is to live out of your RV, not in it. I eat and sit outside a lot. On days off from my various work-camping jobs, I hop in my truck and drive to other locations. I take frequent hikes and walks. I don't often have to worry about cabin fever in the winter, because I winter in places where it's warmer.

It's also true that a small RV requires more downsizing, but there's a beauty to be found in living with less stuff. Everything I own fits in my RV and truck, and no, I never feel wanting for lack of "stuff".

For most Americans, lifestyle inflation is the natural course of life. The more money you make, the more things you buy to show the world your increased status. The more things you have, the bigger the house you need to keep it all in. The larger the house, the more you need to work to afford it, and the less time you actually get to enjoy it all. It's a vicious cycle, and one our consumer-driven economy encourages because it makes the folks at the top more money. Possessions end up owning you instead of the other way around.

Minimalism is the name given to the lifestyle of purposefully owning less, and like full-timing before retirement it's growing in popularity. It's beyond the scope of this guide to cover the whole breadth of minimalism, which is just as common among people who live stationary lives as those who are nomadic, but there are a lot of blogs, forums, and books out there devoted to the topic for those who are curious. Two of my favorite minimalism blogs are listed in the appendix.

I am not a strict minimalist, but I do advocate a simpler way of life. Small RVing is about choosing experiences over possessions. You could spend your hard earned money on items that provide only brief gratification until your neighbor trumps you by getting the next big thing, or you could spend it traveling. When you're on your death bed, do you think you'll be remembering with fondness that entertainment center you bought on sale? Of course not, you'll be thinking of the memories you made, the places you went and the people you met along the way.

I cannot count the number of retired RVers I've met in my travels who wished they would have started on the road when they were younger. I've heard it dozens of times by now. Going small is the answer that will get you on the road sooner, allowing you to live a bigger life full of the kind of memories you'll be glad to have when you reach old age.

2B: Picking your perfect small RV

At this point, when a life of travel finally starts to look possible, people tend to jump right into thinking about how much this is all going to cost. But you can't know what it's going to cost until you do some research on RV options first.

The process looks something like this:
1. Figure out generally what you want in an RV.
2. Look at the sizes, brands, and floor plans available for that type of RV, research and evaluate their usefulness to your unique situation and durability for full-time living–this step will take awhile.
3. Pick the one you like best, and through more research get an idea of what the price tag is generally like.
4. If the price tag is far outside your means, start at step 1 or 2 again keeping that in mind.
5. Finally, if it's reasonable, figure out how to get the money if you don't have it now. We'll cover that later in Part 3.
6. Buy your RV, have fun living the dream.

The easiest way to reach a goal is to make it a concrete, measurable one. Saying "I need to save some money for an RV" is not as powerful as saying "I need to save $1,000 more for the RV I want." This is one reason why you need to pick the RV you want before asking the money question.

The other is because you might very well be disappointed if you

9

simply pick the first RV you can find and afford now without researching all the options. You could discover after you're on the road that for just a bit more money saved you could have bought one you liked a lot better. This is your future home we're talking about, and it absolutely has to meet your personal needs—whether those needs are cheap or expensive to meet—or you're not going to have a good full-timing experience.

So let's talk a little more about choosing an RV by elaborating on steps 1 and 2 from the list above.

There are quite a few small RV options out there. The first decision you need to make is whether you'd rather drive your RV (a motorhome) or tow it behind another vehicle (a towable). If you're a complete newbie to RVs, you can find links to my articles on the different types of RVs with their benefits and disadvantages, listed in the appendix. This is also a good time to turn to The Perfect Small RV Worksheet, also in the appendix.

While you're looking over the different types and weighing their pros and cons (there is no one best type of RV, just the best type for you), you'll want to think on the features and layout of your future home on wheels.

As a full-timer, what amenities are you going to want? It's entirely a matter of personal preference. What you deem necessary is not likely to be the same as the next person, so yes, it's time to put on your thinking cap. Not all types of RV are going to offer everything you may want so this will influence your decision.

As a starting point, here are the amenities my small RV has:
- Toilet
- Shower
- Two sinks
- Gray, black, and fresh water tanks
- Two-burner stove
- Microwave
- A/C unit
- Roof fan
- Awning
- Single, low-clearance axle
- Convertible full-size bed/dinette
- Convertible child-size bed/dinette

And a few things my small RV doesn't have:
- Oven
- Furnace
- Couch
- TV

Whether you decide on a towable or a motorhome, it's crucial that you take your time deciding and be thorough in your search. Class B's, Class C's, conversion vans, pop-ups, and travel trailers can all make viable full-time living quarters and the best way to figure out which small RV will work best for you is to spend time looking at and touring every kind. Visit RV shows, take a trip to your local RV dealer, and pay attention to the RVs you see in campgrounds. When you're touring them, lie down on the beds, sit on the toilets, and mime taking a shower. Look inside every storage cubby and imagine where your belongings will fit.

Just seeing pictures of the interior or layout and a list of features online is not recommended because it's impossible to get a real sense of scale, but once you've narrowed it down a little by looking in person the internet can be really helpful. Search online for communities and forums dedicated to the RV you're interested in and see what owners have to say about it—do they seem generally happy with their decision? What are the common problems seen with this type or brand of RV? Maybe you can even arrange to meet with someone at a rally to give you a tour of their RV. This is especially handy for harder to come by RVs like my Casita that are built to order and won't be found on a dealer's lot.

2C: Taking the scary out of used RVs

It's a topic that causes RV forums to erupt into debate and makes cautious wannabes cringe: whether or not it's worth it to buy used.

By this point in the game, most prospective RVers have learned just enough to realize how complicated RVs are and how little they really know. To anyone in this situation, a new RV sounds like the safer choice. Everything in it should be working and if it isn't, there's a manufacturer warranty that will take care of any issues that pop up.

But the price for new is steep, and not always worth it.

Let me share with you a couple of statistics commonly heralded on the big RVing forums like RV Net and Escapees.

11

1. RVs depreciate much faster than houses or cars. With a few exceptions (like molded fiberglass trailers), a new RV will lose about 50% of its value in five years. When you can get a five year old RV for about half of the cost of a new one, that's a huge difference. In five years, an RV will have all of the new-RV kinks worked out, but will still be in good shape if it's a decent brand and the previous owner(s) took care of it.

2. Half of new full-timers buying their first RV will be in a different RV in two years–and yes this applies to people who opt for small RVs too. This is because no matter how much you research, nothing can eclipse the experience gained by living the lifestyle. So if you decide to buy a brand new RV right off the bat and you're one of those 50%, you're going to lose a considerable amount of money when you resell it.

Then, you always have to remember that companies offer warranties on things because on average the numbers work out in their favor. When I bought my used truck, I took a warranty on it that cost me $1,200 and lasted 20,000 miles. At the time I was feeling pressured to protect my new investment, but after getting home I read the fine print of the warranty, did the math, and got to thinking about it. The odds were that I wouldn't have $1,200 worth of covered repairs on the truck during that time (because if it did routinely work out like that, CarMax would lose money on it, and no business is going to do that intentionally). I called them back a week after purchase and canceled the warranty and got my money refunded, and in the end it was the right choice since I had at most $250 worth of repairs that the warranty would have covered in those first 20,000 miles.

All of those reasons aside, many people on a budget aren't going to be able to afford a new RV anyway; that's the category I fell in. Whether by choice or necessity, buying used doesn't have to be a big risk.

The biggest mistake buyers tend to make is to check the appliances, plumbing, and electrics without checking the body of the RV itself. Leaks and structural integrity are the most important things to look out for in a used RV, as issues with these are the most time consuming and costly to fix–if they even can be.

Water damage is the number one killer of RVs. Once the frame or flooring start rotting out, the cost to repair them is often more than the RV itself is worth given their fast depreciation. Yes, if an appliance like the microwave or A/C doesn't work that can be an annoyance, but these are much easier problems to fix.

Included in the appendix is an Inspection Checklist for used RVs. When you're looking at what might be the RV of your dreams, it's easy to forget about all the things that should be checked so take this list with you and make sure the salesperson or owner goes over the whole list with you. Alternately, if you have the money to spare and want professional advice, you can see about hiring a certified RV technician from a neutral third party to go over the RV for you. Cost might range from $100 to $500 depending on how thorough the check is and how far they have to drive.

Also have a list of questions to ask the owner or dealership when you go, like what optional features the RV has, how long it's been up for sale, if there are maintenance records from the previous owner, and ask to see the manufacturer manuals. These questions are also on the Inspection Checklist for your convenience. Check that the VIN number on the RV is present and legible, and write it down so that you can go home and do some research on the RV yourself before purchasing—and yes, it's a good idea to think overnight on a purchase as big as an RV to let the excitement and emotion die down. This way, you can think critically about how well this RV meets up to the standards you decided on in part 2B.

Few people find The One on their very first outing, so be patient. There are used RVs in good condition out there, it just might take a little while to find the right one.

2D: Dry weight, CCC, and GVWR?

You'll notice as you start shopping around that all RVs are going to have a few different numbers listed. By law it'll be on a sticker somewhere on or in the RV, usually where you find the VIN number. It may also appear in various paperwork you look at:

- A dry weight – how much the RV weighs completely empty without belongings and with all tanks empty
- The CCC – that's Cargo Carrying Capacity, the weight in stuff you can put in the RV

- And a GVWR – which stands for Gross Vehicle Weight Rating, this number is the maximum weight the RV can be fully loaded, basically the dry weight plus the CCC

I know I know, you likely find these numbers as boring and confusing as I did, so I'll try to make this as clear and painless as possible.

A higher CCC will mean you can put more belongings inside your new home. You can't rely on just the number and size of storage bins and cabinets as a marker of how much you can stuff in a RV. Often, RVs will have more storage space than CCC. It's not uncommon to hit that GVWR number while you still have empty cabinet space left, so it's important to keep track of the CCC and GVWR numbers.

It's also important to note that the dry weight listed on the RV might not be the true dry weight. That number is put there by the manufacturer before optional features (like fancy granite counter tops, wood flooring, or even optional amenities like a furnace) are added. Whether buying from a dealer or a private owner, always check to see if any of these things might affect the dry weight listed on the sticker.

Using myself as an example, my trailer's dry weight is 2,200 lbs on paper, but 2,700 in actuality because of the modifications previous owners made before I bought it. (Shortly after buying your RV, you'll want to get it weighed empty, and then you'll want to get it weighed again once it's fully loaded to make sure you don't go over the GVWR.) My trailer's GVWR is 3,500 lbs.

3,500 – 2,700 = 800 lbs

So I have 800 lbs to work with when loading my little home up, and not the 1,300 lbs that the paperwork would have me think. But that's still not the final answer, because the dry weight also assumes that the propane, water and waste tanks are empty, so I really have closer to 600 lbs to work with when the tanks are full.

Why is the GVWR so important to follow? Because that's how much weight the frame, axle(s), and tires are designed to handle. If you overload your little RV, you decrease its lifespan, decrease your fuel economy, and increase the likelihood of blowouts.

Thus concludes the lesson. Hopefully you managed to stay awake for that, because while these numbers aren't sexy or fun, they're a necessary evil for RVers to know.

2E: Demystifying tow vehicles

If you already have a vehicle you want to tow with, look at the owner's manual and see what the maximum tow rating is for that vehicle. The manual will also let you know at what tongue weight you need a weight distribution hitch and/or a sway bar. You may notice that there are multiple tow ratings listed in the manual depending on if you have a tow package or not, so if you aren't sure take a peek under the hood.

Tow packages are very good things for full-timers because of the frequent stress you'll be putting on the vehicle–especially if you plan on driving in the mountains. The two essential things a tow package includes are: 1. The electrical plug that powers your trailer's lights, brakes, and battery charger; and 2: a transmission cooler. If your chosen tow vehicle does not have these, get them installed by a good mechanic ahead of time. There are other things a tow package may include that are not as essential but still handy to have, like a heavy-duty alternator.

Now back to the tow rating. When you're searching for RVs–somewhere between steps 2 and 3 in the RV search list in 2B–make sure the GVWR doesn't go above 80% of the maximum tow rating. And actually, for full-timing, 70% is safer. Why not 100%? First, because the manufacturer tow rating assumes the tow vehicle is empty when towing, which it won't be if you're full-timing. And second, because you're going to be towing frequently which puts a lot of stress on a tow vehicle. It'll hold up better if you don't run it at full capacity.

Using myself as an example again, my Casita has a GVWR of 3,500 lbs. My truck's maximum tow capacity is 6,500 lbs as listed in the manual, including the 'bonus' it gets for having a tow package.

3,500 / 6,500 = 0.53846

So I'm at 53.8% of my truck's maximum tow capacity towing with the trailer full, well below even the 70% threshold. And wouldn't you know it, I've towed over mountain passes at elevations of 10,000+ feet, on 9% grades that lasted seven miles, and never lost my brakes or needed to service my transmission.

On the other hand, if you don't have a vehicle that can tow, turn to The Perfect Tow Vehicle Worksheet in the appendix now. Your RV search procedure will look something like mine did:

1. After deciding on a towable, choose between a pop-up, travel trailer, or hybrid travel trailer.
2. Look at the sizes, brands, and floor plans available for your chosen type. Research and evaluate their usefulness to your unique situation and durability for full-time living–this step will take a while.
3. Pick the one you like best, and get an idea of the usual price range. If it's already too high before thinking about the tow vehicle, start back at step 2 or 3. Otherwise, look at the GVWR.
4. Now look at what size tow vehicle you'll need to pull a trailer with that GVWR without going over 80% of its tow rating. Again, you'll be researching brands and floor plans, but this time for vans, trucks, and/or SUVs.
5. Find the likeliest couple of candidates, and look at their price tags.
6. If the price tag for both the tow vehicle and the RV combined is far outside your means, go back a couple steps again, keeping that in mind.
7. Finally, if it's reasonable, figure out how to get the money if you don't have it now (coming up in Part 3).
8. Buy (or trade in for) the tow vehicle first, then the RV. Have fun living the dream!

The reason why you figure out what RV you want before deciding on the tow vehicle because the RV is the more important of the two. It's what you're going to be living in while the tow vehicle is just a means to an end. You don't want to arbitrarily buy the tow vehicle before doing this research and then discover that it's incapable of towing the RV that meets your needs.

That being said, when it comes time to make the purchases, you'll be buying the tow vehicle before the RV so that you have a way to move the RV. Make absolutely certain you're happy with your RV choice before you buy the tow vehicle that matches it, because once you have the tow vehicle your options are limited by its tow rating.

Part 3
Money

3A: How to calculate how much money you need to go full-timing

A noteworthy observation: Most people will use what they have to buy a RV, whether that's a lot of savings or a little.

When I first gave thought to full-time RVing in December of 2010, I had around $20,000 in the bank. I thought $10,000 for a used Casita and $6,000 for a truck after trading in my car was a reasonable amount to pay (that didn't end up being quite what I paid, but it was close). I already had enough to cover those purchases in the bank, but over the course of 10 months before buying the truck in October of 2011 I saved another $3,500 to give me a better cushion for other RV necessities for starting out.

For someone who has a better paying job and perhaps $40,000 in the bank, they'll likely look for RVs that are more expensive. A good friend of mine had only $7,000 when she started, so she was satisfied with an RV that cost less.

The problem with following this route is one I listed in the previous section; your needs in a home will vary. Some people can be happy in a cheap RV and some simply can't. There's nothing wrong with being the latter, but you'll want to figure this out ahead of time. All too often I've heard of prospective full-timers with stars in their eyes take off with very little planning or research in whatever rig they could get their hands on at the moment. Once they get on the road , they soon realize that their needs aren't being met. These are the folks who get off the road after six months and go back to sticks and bricks living, their options exhausted until they could save up more money to try again.

This is why I insist that all wannabe full-timers research the full-timing lifestyle with its ups and downs (if you follow my blog, you know they exist), and take a good long look at RV options before looking at the money. If you skipped right to this section and haven't thought about what you want in an RV first, go back to Part 2B now. Yes, right now. I'll wait here for you.

...

Back? Okay. Here is the magic formula to discover how much you REALLY need to go full-timing, the calculation I did to choose a number for myself (now would be an appropriate time to look at The Money Worksheet included in the appendix this book).

Pull out that price range you decided on in part 2B. Multiply the highest end by 1.5. This will be your target savings number to get started full-timing.

To return to my own example, Cas was $9,000, Bertha was $6,500 (yes, I've named them) after trade in of my previous vehicle. That's $15,500 total.

$$15,500 \times 1.5 = \$23,250$$

I spent almost exactly 2/3 of my savings on the rig purchase directly. That gave me a good cushion left over for other RVing necessities, like a good hitch and installation of it ($800), a brake controller ($150), hoses, a water filter, and a water pressure regulator ($45ish), leveling blocks and chocks ($40), and a high quality laptop ($1,100).

Throw in taxes and registration, and some left over for the inevitable minor repairs on an older RV, and it put me right around $5,000 left of my original funds. I set that money aside and refused to touch it for regular expenses—that was my emergency fund, which I highly encourage all RVers to have. In the meantime, I was still working my last real job when I was making these purchases, so I didn't need to rely on my savings for my daily living costs.

I cannot possibly cover every single thing that could change this formula, but this gives you a good starting point to think about your own situation and how these numbers relate to you. A few things that might affect your numbers are as follows:

How long will you need to live on savings after you start full-timing?
I had a job lined up that started two weeks after I hit the road as a full-timer, so the fact that I wiped out my savings (aside from my

emergency fund) was planned and accounted for. If you want to travel without working for a while when starting out, multiply the number of months you want to travel without working by your monthly living cost, and subtract that total from your available savings to get started full-timing. Don't know how to calculate your monthly living costs? We'll get to that in the next section.

Related to that, if you have a job lined up for after you hit the road, but are not currently earning a paycheck, then your savings is dropping and you're in a similar situation. Make sure you have enough money set aside for living expenses until departure so that you're not resorting to surviving on ramen noodles in the meantime... unless you're really into ramen noodles that is.

Alternately, if you've purchased a lot of the things you'll need for RVing ahead of time, it's possible you won't need that 1/3 allotment of savings for that side of things.

How much money can you get selling your old stuff?

You'll be trading in your old vehicle to buy your RV, so the trade-in value of your current vehicle (if you have one) gets added to your available savings. Possessions you're needing to sell to fit into an RV (up to and including a house) also ups your purchasing power for the RV if you get it sold beforehand, so you may want to think about downsizing sooner rather than later. For more on downsizing, refer to the appendix.

Will you need to do immediate repairs on your prospective RV?

If you're going to be buying a fixer upper that you plan to restore, a vehicle that you plan to convert into an RV, or any RV that you already know or suspect will need major repairs soon, you'll want to research and get an estimate on those costs and add them to the purchase price before doing your calculation.

For example, let's say that you already have a vehicle capable of towing and the $3,000 travel trailer you're looking at is deeply discounted because the roof is leaking and needs replacing. How much is it going to cost you to fix that? $1,000 is probably not far off. So instead of 3,000 X 1.5, calculate 4,000 X 1.5 to make sure you'll have enough for everything.

Once you've thought through the variables for any possible edits to the formula and done the calculation for yourself, you now have your target number. Congratulations, you're now one very important step closer to realizing the full-timing dream!

If you're not at that target number in savings, there are two paths you could take, and I want to stress than neither is right or wrong: you just need to decide which way is best for you. You can either delay going until you've saved up the money (that topic is up soon), or find a cheaper rig and go now (that topic is up later). But first a little about debt, which might sound like a tempting third option.

3B: Avoiding debt

Once you've had a chance to see the vast number of small RVs out there, it's easy to get lured in by the most expensive of them. If you're visiting dealerships, salespeople will be more than happy to talk to you about financing rigs that are beyond your budget because that's how they make the most money.

One the best decisions I made when I took to life on the road was deciding not to go into debt to buy my rig, and I've never felt disadvantaged by deciding to live within my means.

I've been able to afford 6+ weeks of "vacation" every year I've been on the road. I've been able to work at minimum or near minimum wage most of the year doing seasonal jobs in fun locations and still be able to save up money to travel thousands of miles. That kind of work-life balance is possible because I keep my expenses as low as possible.

Small RVing offers a lot of flexibility. Pick a direction and start driving; there are many wonders in our country to see that don't require reservations, and your smaller rig will fit in more spots than the typical RV will. You're free to change location on a whim if you're not enjoying a place, or extend a stay a few more days if you find something unexpected that really holds your interest. In short, RVing is freedom.

Debt takes some of that freedom away. The more you accumulate in debt trying to get on the road the more your new flexibility will be tempered by it.

There are two major ways by which debt hampers RVing. The first is time or money. To account for that monthly payment, you will have less money to spend on attractions, upgrading your rig, or on gas to travel to a new location. Talk about being a drag on your dreams.

Or you can choose to still do all of the fun things you wanted to do when you hit the road, but then you'll need to find a way to earn more money while you travel to account for that payment. Making that extra money will cost you in free time. If you want to pay off the debt quicker for less interest, that'll mean less enjoyment and more working in the short run. If you want to pay off the debt slower to enjoy your new RVing lifestyle more today, that'll mean less enjoyment and more working in the long run.

Besides money and free time, debt also wears on you mentally. Every time you make a purchase, you'll need to weigh in your head your ability to make that payment. If you keep a strict budget to make sure you have enough money to avoid this pitfall, then it diminishes spontaneity when something unexpected comes up that you want to pursue. You'll have to pass, because it's not in the budget.

The good news is that the initial purchase is the hardest part of the money question. After you have your rig and the initial gear, the costs of full-time RVing are pretty easy to control by staying at campgrounds for longer periods of time at reduced prices and driving less, eating in more, doing activities that don't involve entrance fees, boondocking and choosing lower cost places to stay. It's getting over that initial hurdle that is mostly likely to put people in financial constraints. So up next we'll talk about how to save up for an affordable small RV without going into debt.

If you are already in debt, you're going to have your work cut out for you, but all is not lost. I don't feel qualified to give advice on getting out of debt as I've never dealt with it myself, but I know of two good resources, listed in the appendix. Both were started by people who had a large amount of debt and blogged about their journey to getting debt free. One even traveled internationally and later took a six month RVing sabbatical in the states, proving that being in debt need not be the end of your RVing dreams.

3C: Option 1: Delaying departure to save up more money

Saving money doesn't have to be as hard as traditional financial gurus would have you believe. You can go online and find blogs devoted to personal finances. You could create spreadsheets, take classes, hire an expert, and generally spend a lot of time learning how to save up for a big purchase. Nothing against those options personally, but I prefer to take a cheaper and simpler route:

Spend less than you make.

Okay, I'll elaborate. Here's what to do once you finish the RV searching phase and have a target number to hit for savings.

1. Keep track of all the money you spend in a month, and all that you have coming in. I had always been a saver, and whenever I poked at my bank balance, as long as it went up and not down I was happy. But once I decided that I wanted $3,500 more before hitting the road, a little more planning was in order.

If you need a notebook to write down all your purchases in, do that. For me, I use my debit card for everything and seldom use cash, so it was as easy as checking my online bank statements for a month and adding it all up. When I did use cash, I'd withdraw it using my debit card so it would show up on my statements. Try adding up all your food related expenses for the month, all of your gas, all of your entertainment, all of your personal expenses, etc. into different categories.

2. Do this for a few months while you work on other things, because there will be some variations from month to month as different bills come through. For instance I discovered I always lost money two months out of the year when my car insurance came due. To make it easier to calculate my average savings, I switched my car insurance to a pay every month plan which made it easier to calculate what my monthly savings would be.

3. Think about where you can cut out expenses to save more. Remember that you're going to be hitting the road soon, so there's little point in buying new home decor for the house or apartment. Do you really need to spend money on more clothes when you'll have to get rid of a lot of it to fit in smaller RV closets? Instead of taking a vacation out of town, can you take more frequent weekend trips to local attractions and save more that way? How about eating out less and eating in more? This all may seem like a sacrifice now, but once you hit the road your whole life will be a sort of modified vacation, and reigning in spending now will get you out there that much faster.

4. Is there anything you can do to bring in more money right now? Can you pick up more hours at work? (Just don't burn out trying to do it). Can you do odd jobs in your neighborhood? How about a

garage sale? You now know that you don't need these possessions to be happy, and you'll need to get rid of them to go RVing anyway. Maybe you have a hobby that could bring in a little extra money with some effort, like photography, writing, web design, crafting, programming... there are a lot of options out there.

5. Start downsizing your lifestyle now. Living at my last apartment, I saved maybe $150 a month. At the cheaper apartment I lived in before that, I'd save $200-300 a month. In hindsight it's pretty clear I should have stayed in the cheaper one. If you can do anything to downsize your lifestyle and minimize your monthly expenses right now, it'll help. Sell extraneous vehicles, get the house on the market early and move into an apartment until you hit the road, make a meal plan for the week and manage your grocery buying more efficiently. You plan on living a simpler life on the road, so why not start living simpler now to make living on the road an easier transition?

All of that being said, I understand that personal finance comes easier to some than others. If you're less of a natural saver and find yourself needing more advice, see the appendix.

Once you've targeted and acted on these opportunities for improvement, it's a matter of keeping an eye on your savings and celebrating the milestones. You're now on your way!

3D: Option 2: Take what you have for money and go now

Maybe you're at a point in your life where you just can't wait to go RVing. Maybe you're about to be or have just been laid off. Maybe you've been unemployed for a while due to the poor economy and just can't find another job in your area. Maybe you need to quit your well-paying job to keep from going insane and you know you won't be able to save money after that. Or maybe you know yourself well enough to know that you'll never be able to change your spending habits while still living a traditional lifestyle and only a radical shift will spur you into action.

Even if you have very little money saved up, there are still options. I have met people who've successfully gone full-timing with small trailers that cost $2,000 or less, or old vans that cost $1,000. There are just a few important things to keep in mind if you're thinking about this route:

- Know thyself. While I couldn't fathom living in a 45' RV, there are a lot of RVers that couldn't fathom living in a 17' one. If for instance you can't be happy in an RV that doesn't have a toilet and shower in it, then you can't, and that's that. If you don't have the money for a rig that meets your standards and can't be satisfied living in one that cuts corners until you do, you may have to leave the full-timing dream for a future date and come back to it later.

- Make sure you do a thorough check of the features and quality of any RV that is bargain priced before you buy. You don't want to spend $1,000 on a rig just to have to turn around and spend another $2,000 to get it road worthy (unless you enjoy fixing up things and have the time and money to do it that is). Refer to the used RV checklist included with this guide to help you spot potential problems.

- Even if you do your homework and the RV you're looking at doesn't have any obvious issues when you buy it, it's likely to develop issues sooner rather than later. Be prepared to learn and buy equipment to fix problems yourself as they come up, make friends with the kind of people who can, or start saving up now so you can pay a service center to do it for you.

- These rigs are going to look dated, and sadly it's possible other people, even RVers, will look down on you for having a 'cheap' looking RV. Some privately owned campgrounds and RV parks even have age restrictions and won't let rigs older than a certain year in. It helps to wash the rig regularly and do touch ups on the exterior– just because you're living in an inexpensive RV doesn't mean it has to look bad.

If these potential challenges are things you can live with, then going RVing with very little money can still be a rewarding experience. For further study, see the appendix.

3E: RVing costs once on the road compared to living stationary

Now that you know what you want in an RV and are working on saving up the money to buy it, it's time to think about finances once you're on the road. You've already done half of the work if you've followed my earlier instructions from 3C: you should be looking at your cost of living per month and taking into account how much you're spending on food, entertainment, personal items, bills, rent/housing and gas on a monthly basis. This is important to know, because for most people, their costs for staying on the road are pretty similar to what they were living stationary–whether they lived frugally or in luxury.

We all have habits when it comes to spending, and a lot of these habits don't change just because you hit the road. For instance, you'll still need to eat once you're RVing, and if you had a tendency to eat out five nights a week pre-RVing, you'll likely continue to do so by default unless you make an effort to change that habit.

Likewise your entertainment is probably going to be similar, if you like spending money to go out on weekends, you'll probably still feel pulled to spend money regularly on attractions after you hit the road. People who like eating in and taking walks as their primary form of entertainment will likely still do so once traveling and will continue to spend less.

Other expenses will remain similar because they will be traded off. You'll no longer have rent or a house payment, but instead you'll have campground fees, and campgrounds can be expensive if you want to stay in nice places. The rate for my rented townhouse in Okatie, SC (only two years old, over 1,100 square feet, two bedroom, shared with a roommate) was $417.50 a month for me, or about $13.92 a night. Add in electric at an average rate of $1.70 per day in the height of summer with A/C running all the time (our monthly bills were around $100) and water/sewage at about $0.50 per day and that means that for my new, spacious townhouse in a nice neighborhood not far from the coast I paid about $16.20 a night during the costliest part of the year. Now, the cost for a tent site without even electricity for one night in Zion National Park where I work-camped for a summer was $20. Ouch.

You'll no longer have house or renter's insurance, but instead you'll have RV insurance. Maintenance and repairs is another trade off: RVs are complex structures that are put under earthquake-like stress every time you travel, and even if you buy brand new, something will break sooner or later. Even if it's under warranty, there is still routine maintenance that you will be paying to keep on top of, and to get the most of your investment you'll want to spend the money to keep your RV in good shape even if you pare down costs in other areas.

If your previous residence required a lot of repair, this number may be less once you're on the road, but if you buy an older RV that needs considerable attention, or if you're coming from an apartment where you had a maintenance crew to cover all the costs of repairs like I did, it could very well be more.

Even if living in an RV is less costly than a house or apartment, there is the price of fuel to be considered. You will be traveling in it right? When I first hit the road in September of 2012, I drove 1,228 miles and spent $376.41 on gas in a matter of three days. That adds up fast.

Many new full-timers make the mistake of living like they're on permanent vacation when they first start and that's a good way to blow through a lot of money in a short amount of time. You want to avoid this phenomenon because not only will it deplete your travel fund in a hurry, it'll lead to exhaustion and burn out. Frequently when I was working at my summer National Park jobs I'd talk to vacationing families who were nearing the end of their road trip, and they were so worn out from trying to go everywhere and see as much as possible in their one or two week vacation that they were ready to go back to work and relax. How sad and backwards is that?

So, how do you ensure that your costs on the road are equal to or less than they were living stationary?

As mentioned before one of the great things about full-timing is the flexibility. If you do find yourself spending more money than you would like, it's not too hard to adjust the costs—there are no long-term housing contracts to worry about out here and no need to cram everything in at once. Cook more, avoid tourist traps, rent RV sites monthly instead of daily, travel slower, volunteer in exchange for a free site, and find ways to entertain yourself that don't require wads of cash.

I find hiking and reading outside while I travel to be highly enjoyable and rewarding, and it doesn't cost me a penny. I discovered that traveling at a slower pace allowed me more time to fully explore and get a feel for the places I visited. Rejoice—this is no longer a vacation, it's your life. But to sustain it, you'll need to keep a budget in mind. For more information on how to stay entertained on the road while living frugally, see the appendix.

3F: Earning a living on the road

This is a very complex subject which could easily have a whole book devoted to it. In fact, there are books out there devoted to it, and if you're really stuck about how to earn a living while traveling you'll want to do research beyond the scope of what this chapter offers.

If you already have a job that doesn't require being in one spot, the easiest course is to work on transitioning it to be location independent. If you're working for yourself or as an independent contractor, it's a matter of setting up your business so it can move with you. If you're working for someone, this means negotiating a deal of some sort with your boss.

Examples in this category include software developers, online educators, life coaches, writers, musicians, and transcriptionists... basically, anything you can do that doesn't require the customer (and/or employer) to be there in person, and if it involves physical items, they're small and/or portable enough to take with you in an RV (laptop, phone, smaller craft projects, etc).

And before you write these examples off as fluff jobs that no one really makes any money from, check the appendix where I have listed a real person for each example who makes considerable money from their work and has integrated it with travel. The options are almost endless, and even if you don't currently engage in work that can be made location independent, you'll probably want to start thinking about it for the future.

The great thing about this category of jobs is that they are truly mobile, giving you a lot of freedom to travel how and where you want. Your only restrictions are communication related such as having a phone signal and/or internet connection to keep in touch with your customers or boss, and possibly a post office close enough to mail physical product from if that's part of the business.

If you're anything like me, you've considered this advantage and given this mobile income thing a serious thought. You may have already done some searching about how to earn money online and discovered a slew of scams that made you leery about anything you read online when it comes to work-from-home options..

But there are real opportunities out there, even if you don't want to start your own business. My first foray into the online working waters was with Lionbridge, as an Internet Search Consultant, back in May of 2011. In this very real online working opportunity, you rate

27

the results search engines spit out for a specific query, based on how relevant they are to the query. It's a part time gig, 10-20 hours a week, but for the US job postings, the pay ramped up to $12 an hour once you met their productivity standards (which usually took two months), not bad for a part-time job.

Which brings me to another thing about earning money by working for yourself. A lot of websites or blogs about the subject seem to think that it's an all or nothing deal, and really for most people it isn't. Overnight success stories get a lot of media attention, but few people realize that the folks who make it big through entrepreneurship seemingly overnight have a lot of projects in their past that weren't instant successes. They paid their dues, making mistakes and learning lessons through previous endeavors to gain the knowledge to finally put out that website, service, or product that made it big.

In the real world, I've spoken to a lot more people who had luck making money online by doing a lot of little part time projects, instead of investing in one big one. This has its pluses. Smaller projects can get off the ground more quickly, so even if you aren't making as much money, you make it sooner (why yes, this guide is an example of one such project).

Plus it has the advantage of diversity. If something stops working and one project fails, you still have the other ones to rely on so your income doesn't completely stop. Tomorrow, if Amazon changes its policy and I'm no longer able to earn affiliate income through Interstellar Orchard, I'll still have this book bringing in some change so I'm not completely without pay.

After you get several little projects going, see which one has the best time-to-pay ratio (earns you the most money with the least amount of effort) and focus on expanding on that one, while keeping an eye out for new opportunities.

As to knowing what kinds of projects to invest your precious time and money in—the ones people will pay good money for—there will always be some uncertainty. It's the nature of the game.

- Start with a list of things you enjoy doing, because entrepreneurship requires a lot more effort than working for someone else and if you don't enjoy it, it's likely you won't take the project far enough that you to actually earn money from it (I blogged on IO for 18 months before I made a penny from it).

- Now look at that list and cull things that other people aren't interested in/wouldn't pay you for. Sometimes this is a matter of framing your project in a certain way. For instance, no one is going to pay me for traveling around the country sightseeing. But they will pay me to teach them how to travel around the country and sightsee themselves. If you're still not sure if people would pay you for your idea, look around and see if people are looking for the item or solution you're going to offer. (There are always people on RVing forums asking questions about full-timing).

- Treat your new project like a business if you want it to end up being one. Work on it regularly, establish a rapport with your customers, and put out the best product or service that you can. For informational businesses like IO, that means being as helpful as you can. If you're making a physical product, make sure it's high quality. If you're working in a field with a lot of competition, you'll want to distinguish your work from everyone else's. Corporations thrive on conformity, but small businesses thrive on individuality. (Plenty of people blog about full-timing, but few people blog about how to go full-timing as a young, single woman debt free).

With that as food for thought to get you thinking about location-independent work, let's turn to the second category of jobs, the kind that enabled me to go full-timing.

This second category is jobs that require you to be in one spot. These jobs equate to slower travel, staying in one place probably for months at a time, but you'll also spend less since you can take advantage of monthly rates, won't be using as much gas, and possibly can even get your site and utilities covered by your employer. There are several options here.

1. You could work for a nation-wide company that will allow you to transfer between locations. Home Depot and the Dollar Store are examples that allow transfers like this. I also have one RVing friend who works as a merchandiser for Ace Hardware and he travels with a team that renovates stores. He says the hours are long, but there are gaps between locations for relaxation and the pay is good.

2. If you've got a specialized or trade skill of some sort, you could also

potentially take that on the road. Say you're a plumber. Setting up your own traveling plumbing business isn't really practical, because you won't remain in one spot long enough to build up a reputation and because you won't be able to offer a guarantee on your work that lasts beyond when you leave. But you can always look for contract work with a larger company that does have a presence in the area and can honor a warranty beyond your departure date. Traveling nurses work sort of the same way. You'll be looking for a temporary position, offering relief for permanent employees off on maternity leave or vacation.

3. Temporary or seasonal jobs are one of the easiest ways to make a living on the road. There are a growing number of companies that offer job positions that are catered expressly to RVers (work-camping jobs), and plenty of those jobs are entry level and don't require any experience or schooling.

This is how I got started. Back in July of 2012, I was hired by Amazon's CamperForce program after submitting an application and doing a phone interview–two months before I quit my last stationary job and hit the road. Getting it all set up like that ahead of time gave me a good confidence boost to start full-timing, because it was a solid opportunity with a high earning potential for a temp job. I knew however bad things could possibly be in the month I was traveling before I got to Kansas, at least I'd be bringing in a decent amount of money once I got there.

However, opportunities like Amazon are not the norm. The majority of traditional work-camping jobs are hosting positions at campgrounds. For these jobs you usually exchange a lower number of hours worked a week for the cost of your camp site and utilities. They won't pay the entire cost of your living, but if you have enough money saved up already, or if you're earning money in other ways at the same time, it's definitely worth a look.

If you're not independently wealthy, you'll want to filter through listings of work-camping jobs for ones that offer a 40-hour work week with all hours paid plus a discount on your campsite. These are the ones that offer something closest to a living wage. I've listed the three sites I use to find work-camping jobs in the appendix, plus two blog posts I've written about working at National Parks and for Amazon.

My last bit of advice when it comes to working on the road is to enjoy yourself. Don't get so busy making a living that you forget to make a life, as the saying goes. Whether you take seasonal jobs, work for yourself, or some combination of the two, RVing allows a lot more flexibility for the work/life balance, and there will still be plenty of adventure and fun to be had even though you need to keep working to fund this amazing lifestyle.

Part 4
Small RVing Answers

4A: How to organize and make the most of your limited space in a small RV

In the beginning, the biggest concern is simply getting everything you think you'll need in the RV so you can vacate your residence on time. Downsizing is something all RVers big and small will have to face and if you're looking for more advice, you can read the blog article I wrote about it listed in the appendix.

It's likely your little RV will be very packed with things you discover you never use and don't really need. To keep progressing, continue getting rid of things even after you're on the road. If you go three months without using something (unless it's an item that's necessary for another season), find a way to get rid of it.

Also continue rearranging once you've been traveling a while. Things that you find yourself using frequently, move to more convenient locations. I'm still doing this even after two years. Keep those less-accessible or harder to reach crannies for the things you use only occasionally. Most RV storage compartments are too deep, and if you put things you use frequently in the back, you'll have to pull all the stuff in front out to get to it which gets tiring after a while.

It's also quite possible to forget what you have back in deep storage, even in a small RV. To keep things truly organized, make a list of everything you have stored in every compartment. This way locating things is easy and you won't re-buy things that you already have (Yes, this has happened to me). After making that list, just keep up with it and put things back in their proper place after use.

And yes, you'll want a spot to store everything. A small RV seems a lot more spacious if everything is tucked out of sight behind a cabinet door or in a bin. It gives the illusion of having more room. Even just one item out of place can make the whole space feel cluttered and messy. I've found that I feel less stressed when things are put away and look clean, which is funny because I wasn't particularly neat when I lived in an apartment. Somehow in a space this small, greater cleanliness has become more important.

On the topic of space and storage, in a small RV, every bit of space counts. If there are storage areas that you aren't fully using (and the way most are manufactured, there probably will be), you're wasting valuable resources. Take a look at your cabinets and storage. Nearly always you'll have a couple of cabinets that aren't the right shape for what you want to put in them.

About the easiest modification to make in an RV to increase storage space is to buy bins or put up shelves or dividers to better use the space you have. Below one of my small dinette seats I have a tall but shallow storage space that backs up against one of the wheel wells. I bought two small Rubbermaid office type storage drawers–the kind that has four small shelves stacked on each other–and I put small things like screws, nuts, pens, and nail polish in there. The closet in my Casita used to be a hanging closet, but I can fit a lot more clothing in there with the shelving I have in place.

If you regularly take a little time to keep your storage compartments organized, continue getting rid of items you're no longer using, use shelving and plastic containers to reduce dead space, and keep the living area clear, you'll find you have plenty of room. Oh, and when it comes to space for you, don't forget to follow the advice in section 2A about living out of your small RV instead of in it.

4B: Cooking in a small RV

Cooking on the road can be as simple or complex as you want to make it.

If you enjoy cooking, never fear. Just because your cook and prep space are going to be limited doesn't mean you have to give up enjoying good meals. Finding ways to better utilize your smaller space is the name of the game.

Prep space becomes any available horizontal surface: the small dinette table, the mini counter over the fridge, and even the lid of the stove, which on my RV will flip out and down to give more space to work on. Sometimes you might need to have two distinct phases to your cooking, prep and then clean up so that there is room for the actual cooking.

My Casita has no oven. It does have a two burner stove, but the burners are close enough that only by using two small pots or pans can I have them both going at once. My big saucepan and pot are too large to let the other burner be used. Many small RVs are going to have a similar setup, requiring a little creativity to find a way to prepare meals.

One way to get around this handicap is to focus on meals that can be made in one pot. There are still lots of wonderful things you can cook in one dish.

Another is to supplement your cooking space with electric appliances. For instance, I had one solo RVer friend who used an electric wok to do most of her cooking. Crock pots are another popular choice since they'll cook the food while you're busy doing other things and don't take up a lot of space. I received a tiny George Foreman grill as a gift when I started full-timing that stored very well under the sink when not in use. Most small RVs come with a microwave for simpler food prep, but if you're missing your oven, you have the option to replace the microwave with a toaster oven.

Also don't forget that many small RVs have electrical plugs on the outside, and many RVers will carry camping grills and do the cooking outside on a picnic table when the weather is nice. That gives you more room to work in and also keeps the inside of the RV from getting dirty.

On busy sight-seeing or work days, finding the time and energy to cook can also be a challenge. When I was working at Amazon and had very little free time, I discovered one good way to eat well and yet not have to worry about cooking on full days was to cook large meals ahead of time and then have several days of leftovers.

For this method, focus on dishes that will keep in the fridge. Standard sized Tupperware might not have the dimensions to fit in a small RV fridge well, so I got in the habit of storing non-liquid leftovers in resealable bags. They can be molded to fit in the little nooks and crannies of the fridge that would otherwise be wasted. You can also use this method for storing non-perishables that come in large unwieldy boxes, like cereal.

On travel days, I'm usually on the road most of the day, so I don't have access to my microwave and don't feel like firing up the stove after a long day of driving. To make things easy on myself, I plan ahead and pick up refrigerated food that doesn't require heating up, like potato salad, yogurt, tuna salad, that sort of thing. It's more filling than having cold cut or PB&J sandwiches twice a day but doesn't require more effort.

If you're going to be camping in remote areas where getting to a grocery store is an effort, keep that in mind. Stock up on non-perishables before you get out to the boonies to lengthen your stay. With a bit of extra planning, you won't go wanting on your trip.

Happy cooking, and for more advice, see the plethora of helpful comments on my cooking post in the appendix.

4C: Small RV, cold weather

Having a small RV in cold weather isn't much different than a larger one. In fact it could be considered an advantage with less space to heat and less places for the heat to leak out from. But since the vast majority of small RVs are not designed for winter weather, there are precautions to take.

Keeping yourself warm

If your little RV has a furnace, great. They aren't the most fuel efficient or quiet, but they get the job done.

If you don't, you can still go camping in cold weather–and it doesn't need to cost a fortune. My first December working in Kansas, all I had was a small electric heater that plugged into an outlet and had two intensity settings for heat. It was $20 at Walmart. You had to keep things three feet from the front of it and it really dried out the air (a bonus if you're wintering somewhere damp), but it was effective without the potential of carbon monoxide poisoning.

In my case, I kept it pointed at my bed, and the air around my sleeping space stayed about 30 degrees warmer than outdoors. Inside the bathroom and closed cabinets, and near the windows and walls it was cooler. That's fine and dandy when it's 45 degrees outside, but when it's 25 degrees outside that meant I was only getting up to about 55 degrees inside, which for some people is still awfully chilly. My second December in Kansas was much colder, so I bought a second small space heater which together with the original one could keep the inside 50 degrees warmer than outside. On the three nights it dipped into single digits I was in the upper 50's inside.

There are other heater options out there, some of which could keep a small RV warmer than my little electric ones can. When I get the chance to go boondocking, I believe I'm going to want an Olympian Wave 3 Catalytic Heater. It's a couple hundred dollars and runs off of propane, but it heats much better without the possibility of setting things in front of it on fire, although a vent or window does need to stay cracked to prevent carbon monoxide build up. In the end, most RVers who camp regularly during the winter end up using a combination of propane and electric heaters to keep their RVs warm inside.

Now that you've got some heat running inside your RV, let's keep it there. One of the big places that RVs lose heat is through the windows, especially if your RV doesn't have double-pane windows. Stretching cellophane or cling wrap over them to create a second layer will help a little, but Reflectix does an even better job. Reflectix is shiny on both sides and has the consistency of bubble wrap. You can find it at home improvement stores, RV supply stores, and online. Since it's got some thickness it does a better job of holding heat in, and in the summer it can be put up in windows that receive direct sunlight to reflect the sun away and keep the trailer cooler inside. I had received Reflectix covers for all my windows when I bought my trailer, and when I put them up it makes a noticeable difference in how warm my RV stays with the heater running.

Putting covers or plastic over your other vents, skylights and AC will help too. I didn't know about this trick that first year, but I've done it for cold-weather camping ever since. Just remember to keep a window or vent clear enough that you can open it a little if you're using a propane heater.

Keeping your plumbing warm

Besides keeping yourself warm, you'll also need to think about keeping the plumbing and tanks warm. When liquids freeze into solids, they expand. If there is no room for them to expand, there is the possibility that pipes will burst or connections will start leaking. To keep this from happening, you either need to make sure that your pipes don't freeze, or that they're empty enough that there is room for the liquid to expand when it freezes.

If you're expecting temperatures just a few degrees below freezing for just a couple of hours during the coldest part of the night, you probably don't need to do anything with your plumbing, since it takes a while for water to freeze. If you want to be safe, you can

36

disconnect your water hose for the night and drain it. Where I wintered in northern Florida, forecasters would put out deep freeze warnings when temps of less than 27 degrees were expected for at least two hours, and it was at that point that people were encouraged to take precautions for unprotected water lines.

While some higher end RVs have entirely covered tanks and pipes and heated basements designed to keep things from freezing up, most small RVs are not going to have these luxuries and so you will need to do some prep to be able to handle freezing weather.

The cheapest way to handle freezing weather is just to dump your tanks and unhook your fresh water hose when the overnight forecast is calling for freezing temps. That way even if your tanks and sewer pipes are exposed outside and freeze a little there won't be enough liquid in them to do any harm. It may be inconvenient, but it's hard to argue with free! I highly discourage keeping your black and gray sewer valves open all the time to let them continuously drain, because then liquids drain out of your tanks and leave the solids behind to build up, which can cause blockages and odors after a while, especially for the black tank. The best thing is to dump your tanks when they are getting full. If your tanks aren't very full but still full enough that you might worry about freezing, run water into them first to fill them more before dumping.

This method works well, but what if it stays below freezing long enough that you need working fresh water?

Dripping a line is an option, and it's a simple process and also free (unless you're paying for water by volume). Running water freezes less readily than still water, so leave a sink faucet running at a steady drip to keep the water in your lines moving. The faster you let it run, the less likely it is to freeze, but the faster you'll fill your gray tank too. If you go this route, you will want to keep your gray tank sewer valve open. Since it's going to be pure water without any solids, it should be fine. The biggest problem you can run into with this method is that once it gets cold enough, you won't be able to run the water fast enough to keep it from freezing, particularly on the sewer side of things.

To prevent this, you can buy pipe insulation that can be wrapped around your pipes and hoses. This is still a relatively inexpensive solution. Try to be sure that the spouts and hose connections are protected by insulation on both the RV and sewer side as well as well as the hoses. This won't help your tanks, but those won't freeze as quickly since it's a larger volume.

If it gets really cold, you can purchase heat tape from a hardware store to wrap the hoses and pipes in, though it won't be cheap. When I was looking at heat tape my second winter working in Kansas, 30 feet cost around $42 online for the cheapest brand I could find. Unlike regular insulation, heat tape actively produces heat, but it requires plugging in to a standard 20 amp outlet to work. The best way to use it is to plug it into the pedestal outside and then wrap it over the plumbing. You can put insulation over top for added effect but be careful what kind you use, because the heat produced can melt the insulation. I used ¾" inch pipe foam insulation purchased from Walmart. It was a few bucks for 12' of the stuff in 3' sections and had adhesive on it already which reduced the amount of duct tape needed to hold it together.

If you're one of the lucky ones who has enclosed holding tanks on your small RV, you can run a small incandescent light bulb on an extension cord into the compartment with your holding tanks to produce heat in there. I've heard that there are heating elements meant specifically for the holding tank bays, so that might be worth looking into. In my Casita the fresh water tank is enclosed and there is a way to run a bulb in there, but the gray and black tanks are exposed.

My solution was to stop using the black and gray tanks once daytime temperatures no longer got above freezing. I used the campground bathroom facilities exclusively, and did my dishes in a plastic dishpan. The dirty dish-water would get dumped directly into the sewer drain outside. If you have exposed tanks and you still want to use your waste tanks in freezing weather, consider skirting the bottom of your RV. This keeps the wind from blowing underneath it and will hold in heat. Again you can consider putting some safe, small heating source down near the side where your tanks are.

Even if your tanks are enclosed, some people skirt their RVs as a way to keep cold air from seeping into the interior of the RV from underneath. Most people use commercially-bought skirting from a home improvement or RV supply store. However, if you're handy you could cut boards or vinyl siding to fit, or even just buy heavy plastic sheeting to tape on (though you'll need to weigh down the ends to keep the wind from blowing under it).

One problem with skirting though, is that it may trap moisture down there. If you noticed mold or mildew, you can try keeping one piece of the skirting loose enough so that you can open it up to vent when the weather isn't as cold, or buy disposable packets that absorb moisture.

4D: Pets in a Small RV

Often I talk to people who are interested in small RVing, but reluctant to make the leap because of their pets. Depending on the personality and activity level of the pet, taking them along might not be as hard as you think.

I've met plenty of people who've traveled with pets in their small RV. My first year at Amazon, my neighbor had a converted cargo truck that had less living space than my Casita, and he traveled with his dog Gulliver, who was a good forty pounds. A well-known blogger, RV Sue, travels in her 17' Casita with two rat terrier mixes Spike and Bridget. I lived for over three months in my Casita with my best friend Julie and her cat Fish. Glenn over at ToSimplify lived with his cat Emily in two different class B vans for a total of three years until she passed away from natural causes.

So it's definitely possible. The first consideration is your pet's temperament and activity level.

RVing does favor laid-back personalities with more sedate activity levels. If your pet falls into this category, you're less likely to have issues than someone whose pet is hyper, aggressive, fearful, or prone to motion sickness.

If your pet is very active, plan on more time for walks and outdoor play since they'll have less room inside. You probably won't want to leave them cooped up in the RV for long periods of time. If they're prone to motion sickness, there are medications you can get from a vet to help, but that might not be viable for long-term traveling. If your pet is aggressive towards other animals or people you'll need to take great care in campgrounds that they don't get away from you.

Beyond that, there's the space issue.

In such small quarters it's important to make sure your pet gets enough mental stimulation and exercise, even if they aren't particularly active. Luckily, traveling can help with both. Taking your dog for more frequent walks not only gives you both exercise, it also gives you ample opportunity to explore your temporary home port, and the fact that your location changes gives your pet exposure to new things regularly. Cats might not go for walks, but I think everyone I've met who has traveled in an RV with their cat has leash trained, or at least purchased a collapsible enclosure that could be set up outside to give the cat something to look at that isn't the small interior of their RV.

Having room for all of your pet's stuff is another point to consider. While a food and water bowl might not take up much space in a small RV, finding an out of the way place for a cat's litter box can be challenging. In my Casita, Julie made a litter box out of a plastic storage bin that had walls of the right height to fit underneath the full size bed at the back of the RV. A door was cut out of one side to allow Fish to get in and out. A commercial covered litter box wouldn't have fit under there, but with a little ingenuity we came up with a solution.

Then there's the breed issue.

It is true that there are RV parks out there that have dog breed restrictions, but there are still plenty of options for camping with large or supposedly "aggressive" breed dogs. You'll want to investigate private parks before arriving as those are the most likely to have restrictions. State and public parks though are less likely to be strict about breed, and of course if you're boondocking your pooch won't be a problem at all.

National parks are a mixed bag. Size and breed matter little and in most of them your dog is welcome in the car with you and to stay in the RV in designated campgrounds, but they are usually not allowed in public areas or on trails. If you are going to be visiting a National park with a dog, you may need to look into a pet sitter if you want to spend long periods exploring outdoors.

Once you've assessed the situation and decided that your pet could be compatible with small RVing, it's time to talk about how to introduce them to it. The best way is to do it in stages, if you can manage it. Try bringing the pet out to the RV for a few hours and letting them explore without moving it. If that goes okay, try taking them for a weekend away in it. You need to get the pet to see it is a positive experience, so if they have a favorite toy or treat, bring that along. If you have a shy or skittish pet, or one that hates changes, take the introduction process slowly.

Oh, and one last thing. If you're pulling a trailer, let me make a case for keeping the pet up with you in the tow vehicle while in transit. Trailers bounce around a lot while being towed, which can be stressful and even cause injuries if your pet loses its footing, and a trailer cannot be climate controlled well while in motion. If something should happen to your pet, you wouldn't be aware of it until stopping, which could be hours.

Part 5
Solo RVing Answers

5A: Solo RVer safety

As a young woman traveling alone, I get asked a lot about safety on the road. People often feel worried on my behalf, that I am taking a huge risk living this way and some day it will come back to haunt me.

When I was a college student living in an apartment complex next to campus, a girl coming back from class one afternoon got held at knife point in our parking lot by some members of a gang. They thought she was affiliated with a rival gang. Turns out she was just in the wrong place at the wrong time and they let her go unharmed before the authorities showed up. I was at class when this happened, but it could have been me on a different day.

The point I'm trying to make is, I don't feel like the world is any less safe on the road than it is off. There are risks no matter what lifestyle you choose to live. The only way to insulate yourself from all risk is to avoid getting out and living at all.

The most often expressed concern, especially if you're female, is for your personal safety against 'bad people'. Because stories of violence are so often reported to the public, it can sound like these bad people are all over. They aren't. Most people are good, although random acts of kindness rarely make the headlines.

Since I started RVing, I've been on the receiving end of many random acts of kindness– especially from my fellow RVers. I've been invited over for dinner, loaned tools to perform work on my RV, and when my electrical system stopped working at the first campground I was staying in, my neighbor (whom I'd never talked to before) came over to peek at my fuses and breakers to see what the problem was.

I've had help replacing my tank vents when they were leaking, help replacing my water heater's anode rod when I thought it was rusted in too tight for me to move, help replacing one of the friction pads on my fancy hitch when it wore out and needed changing, and help reattaching a cabinet door that came off in transit. About 40% of the time when I'm hitching or unhitching my RV in a place where people are around, someone will walk over and ask if I need help. Even though I actually prefer no help for this activity, it just goes to show how nice most people are.

On the other end of the spectrum, I've never once had a run in with a 'bad person'. I've over-nighted at truck stops and in Walmart parking lots dozens of times with nary an issue. This makes my parents cringe, but really I'm not tempting danger to come and find me. Most of what keeps you safe on the road is common sense. The majority of my advice is geared toward women since that's where my experience lies, but there are a few things in here that are applicable to guys as well.

When you get to a new RV park, get to know your neighbors. Let them and the main office know that you are alone, and since most RVers are friendly people, they'll likely keep an eye out for you and perhaps even feed you–it's happened to me more than once. If you can't travel directly with someone, then maybe you can caravan along with other RVers, each in your own RV. If you go out hiking or some other activity that takes you away from other people, let someone know or at least carry your phone with you.

Avoid rest stops or staying in parking lots or campgrounds that are empty. If someone unsavory pulls in, there won't be any witnesses to keep them on good behavior. When over-nighting outside of a campground, choose parking lots that are well lit, and park under the lights where security cameras can see you easily. Always lock your door at night. Keep aware of your surroundings when in an unfamiliar place. If you pull in somewhere and get a gut feeling that something is off–move on. As an RVer that's one of your best defenses: your house has wheels, so when something or someone is making you uncomfortable, just keep driving until you find a better spot.

Besides matters of common sense, there are other things you can do as a solo lady to help you feel safer on the road.

For starters, if you're just starting to look at small RVs and are really concerned about safety, consider a van or Class B over a towable. That way you won't need to get out of the vehicle at the end of the day to get from the driver's seat to your living quarters.

Mace or an air horn are good things to carry with you, but be sure to keep them in an easy to reach place so you can get to them quickly. Neither will do you much good buried at the bottom of your purse. Consider investing in a big flashlight that can also double as a weapon when you need to go out at night. Bringing your dog on the road with you (even a smaller breed) can also reduce the chances of being bothered.

A firearm is an option too, but if you go this route please look up gun laws in your domicile state and the states you'll be visiting. Carrying a firearm across state lines can be very complicated, and I'm not an expert since I don't own one so I don't know what the legalities are.

I have also heard of women who have used decoys as a way to deter would-be assailants. For instance putting hunting decals or pro-gun stickers on a tow vehicle, leaving a pair of big men's boots or a large pet bowl and chain outside the RV door at night. I even heard of a woman who had an inflatable doll that sat in the passenger seat of her tow vehicle, dressed up in a flannel shirt and cap. I would consider all of this unnecessary, but if it makes you feel better then that's what's important.

5B: Loneliness

Another major point of resistance I hear from single people who want to go RVing is that they're worried about loneliness. Living alone is one thing, but then when you're traveling you don't get to build a social network like you can living in one spot. Some folks even assume I'm lonely all the time, just because I travel by myself (I'm not).

It's true that loneliness can make what would otherwise be a fun and exciting adventure feel like it's missing something. Before addressing how to combat loneliness on the road though, we first need to talk about the difference between loneliness and being alone, personality types, and conversation types.

Being alone is not the same thing as being lonely. In fact, just about everyone benefits from having some time to themselves every day. The ideal amount of time spent with others varies from person to person. At one point, terms like introverted and extroverted were used to describe whether someone generally preferred their own company or that of others, but now it's more widely understood that introverts and extroverts both need some of both. The real difference is that introverts recharge their batteries so to say with alone time, and extroverts recharge their batteries by interacting with others.

I dislike labels, because they tend to make complex issues seem black and white. To me, it looks like a scale. On one end of the spectrum you have very outgoing people who are always seeking the company of others, who feel the best when they're with a crowd and hate to be alone. On the other end of the spectrum you have those individuals who spend the majority of their lives alone, only rarely do they enjoy the company of others and then preferably only on a one on one basis. But there is a big wide range of possibilities between those two extremes, and I feel most people fall somewhere in the middle. To muddy the distinction even further, it is rare to always fall at the same point on the scale every day, by which I mean that some days/weeks/seasons you may desire more or less interaction with others than you usually do.

American society tends to favor the outgoing personalities over the introspective ones, but both are natural and normal, phobias and anxiety disorders aside. No matter which end of the spectrum you generally fall on, it's possible to make solo full-time RVing work for you, as long as you're willing to put the effort in. This is really the answer to any facet of the full-timing equation you may be stuck on: as long as you're passionate enough about it to put in the work, you'll find a way to make it a reality.

So, have I ever felt lonely while I've been on the road? Most of the time no, but it does happen occasionally. I'm not sure there is a person out there who hasn't felt lonely at some point in their life. In fact it's possible to be in a crowd of people and still feel lonely if you feel like you have little to talk about or common interests to share. Which brings me to the next important point, which is the kind of interaction you're looking for with others.

Some people thrive off of deep conversations, where you discuss your dreams and desires, your likes and dislikes, things that move you, deeply held beliefs, stuff like that. And on the other end some prefer to keep it more superficial, talking about the weather, what you had for lunch that day, or about upcoming travel plans.

In our society, when you're meeting someone for the first time it's normative to stick to superficial conversation, and if you ask someone you don't know well a deep question they are likely to get uncomfortable. Most conversations start with superficial topics, and then as you get to know a person better over a period of time you may choose to get into deeper conversations. Though as we all know not all relationships progress like that.

Now I bet all of us have at least a couple people, family members or close friend with whom we share those deep bonds, but in general some will crave deeper conversation and some won't. There is some theorizing that people who tend more toward the extrovert side of things prefer to stay more on the superficial end of the conversation pool, making small talk with a lot of different people, and those who identify as introverts prefer deeper connections but with fewer people, but again that's just more labeling and not very important to the topic of combating loneliness.

Again, it's not right or wrong to prefer one type over another, it's just important to note that there is a difference and that difference will influence how you go about meeting your social needs on the road.

Whether you fall more towards introvert or extrovert, whether you prefer deeper or more superficial conversation, there are two big areas to focus on when it comes to interaction with others.

First is staying in touch with people you already know. These days cell phones and the internet have made it easier than ever to keep in touch with loved ones, but that doesn't mean it's going to happen automatically.

When I started full-timing, I was a bit surprised at how difficult it was to keep up with some people. Your schedule may be quite different than it was when you were stationary, making it harder to match up your free time with their free time. Plus, if you have a blog or are active on social media, friends of yours may keep up religiously with that and thus feel like they're all caught up with what you're doing without having to talk to you. The problem with that is you aren't getting any time in with them.

The key is to be more proactive. If they won't talk or e-mail you, then you'll have to take the first step. Plan time into your week to call or write to people. Keep their snail mail addresses on hand and send postcards as you travel. Let them know that just because you've moved on to a different phase in your life doesn't mean that you don't still want to stay friends with them.

Even when you make your best effort, it's a sad truth that not all relationships will survive the distance. Some friendships may have been founded on being coworkers, or being in book club together, or some other part of your life that you're done with now that you're traveling, and without that common bond there's nothing to talk about. Other people just need face-to-face contact, and will find it difficult to keep up by less personal means.

Understand that this is a natural part of life. Even if you take traveling out of the picture, people change over time, and so too does the company they keep. Chances are you don't have all the same friends now that you had ten years ago, just because of the ebb and flow of jobs, interests, and hobbies you've had during that time. Change can be scary, but try to look at it as a good thing. That hole in your social life left by those people who aren't traveling will soon be filled by new people you're meeting on the road.

RVing gives you the unique opportunity to meet a lot of different people, from all walks of life. If you're naturally outgoing, it shouldn't be too hard for you to get a conversation going and start making a new friend.

If you're more shy, there's still hope. For starters it shouldn't be too difficult to start up conversations with other RVers you'll be meeting at campgrounds, because you're guaranteed to have at least a shared interest in travel and RVs. In the RVing world, sitting outside on your porch while parked at a site is like an unspoken invitation for other campers to come say hello. After saying hello, just start by asking where they are from, where they are headed, or about some well-known attraction in the area that you've seen or are going to go see. You can also inquire about their RV; most RVers are very proud of their rigs and happy to talk about them. From there the conversation will probably turn up other common interests to talk about.

You can also try chatting up people you meet at various attractions as you travel, if you're looking for more casual conversation. Again, talking about your current location would be a safe way to start a conversation without seeming too forward.

If you're planning to work camp as you travel like I do, you'll have coworkers and possibly guests/customers to get to know. And again, the chances are good that most of your coworkers will be interested in travel. If money isn't an issue for you and you're not planning to work camp, you might want to consider doing occasional volunteer work as you travel. Not only does that open up the same opportunity work campers have for interacting with others, you also get the satisfaction of doing a good deed—helping out in the community you're visiting.

For those people needing deeper interaction, it helps to be an instigator. If you're getting along well with coworkers or other people in the RV park, but the friendship has plateaued, be the one to invite them along on an outing, or over to your place for dinner or a game. Not everyone you meet on your adventure will be game for these deeper conversations, but you'll never find the ones who could be if you don't make an effort. The more people you interact with, the more chances you'll have to find people that you are compatible with. Make the effort early and often, and it'll pay off down the line.

Remember in Part 2B when I brought up joining an online RV community or forum as a way to help you learn more about the RVs out there? Well those connections will serve you well here too. If you get to know someone online, it makes meeting them in person when your paths cross on the road much easier than starting a conversation cold with someone you don't know. While you won't have contact with these mobile friends on a daily basis like you would with a more stationary existence, when you do meet up after a long absence you'll have a lot of catching up to do and adventures to share. Which brings me to a final important point.

Your house is going to have wheels, and that means you'll get to be where you need to be, when you need to be. There is no rule that says you need to immediately hop to the other side of the country when you become a full-timer, and no rule saying you can't come back to visit and catch up with family and friends or even have a 'home port' of sorts to base your travels out of in the event that you decide you need a more stable support network than what you can find solely on the road. You have not 'failed' as a full-time RVer if you do either of these things. Everyone's definition of 'full-timer' is a bit different and the very best thing you can do is mold the term to fit your needs, not the other way around.

As for my own story, a few months after I got on the road in 2012 this was the biggest problem I faced. At Amazon there isn't much opportunity for conversation while on the clock, and the cold weather meant meeting other work campers staying in the park was challenging because everyone stayed huddled in their RVs with the heat on. I'm more of an introvert, and deeper interaction with fewer people is what I need to be most happy. At Amazon on my lunch breaks I was only getting very light superficial conversation with coworkers during lunch and on break, and it wasn't enough for me. By the time I realized that something needed to change, I was already in a bit of a funk since those deeper friendships take longer to build.

That first winter I had promised my parents I'd be home for Christmas before I even became a full-timer in September, but I ended up being doubly glad for the decision. Going back to Wisconsin for those three weeks gave me time to charge back up socially and plan on how to do things differently next time.

The next summer when I worked at Badlands National Park, I had no problems with loneliness. I made the effort to invite coworkers out hiking with me very early on and became friends with several of them. When I returned to Kansas that fall to work at Amazon again, I made the effort early on and it paid off.

Going RVing alone does not have to mean a lonely existence, as long as you know your needs and are proactive about getting out and getting them met.

5C: Having to do it all yourself

When couples go RVing, they develop a routine. The total labor is split between a team with both people sharing the load. Well, as a solo RVer you'll have to do it all. It can be a daunting prospect, but here's another area where choosing a smaller and simpler RV helps. The fewer gadgets on an RV, the less there are to break down. The smaller it is, the less time it'll take to wash the outside and keep it clean on the inside.

Being a solo RVer might force you into doing things that you don't have much experience or desire to do. You'll be pilot and navigator. You'll be housekeeping, head chef, and mechanic. You'll be the travel planner, tour guide, and if you're work-camping, chief job finder.

I was not a particularly handy person before I got on the road. In fact I'd never so much as changed a tire, or the oil in my car, yet somehow I still manage to fix things that go wrong with my Casita on my own. Juggling all of these new roles requires patience with yourself, and a willingness to learn. I found that my willingness to learn stemmed from my intense desire to travel and live life on my own terms. If you're similarly motivated–and I have to imagine you are having purchased this guide–it makes the less desirable parts of RVing more tolerable.

As for the actual "How To", that's what Google and your RV manuals are for. For instance, take mechanical problems. When something goes wrong (and it will, eventually) stay calm. Getting upset or angry at the world won't do you any good and won't get the problem fixed. Check the internet and your manuals for an explanation of how to fix whatever happened. Find a YouTube video. Ask in your RV forum for advice from others with your type of RV. It's likely some of them will have had the same problem, and might be able to tell you how they fixed it. If it sounds like something you can't fix yourself, then it's time to look up repair shops in your area.

If it does sound like something you can fix, dither for a little while, worry about making the problem worse (you probably won't), and finally fix it. Then feel the relief and satisfaction that comes from having solved the problem on your own.

This process can be applied to any aspect of RVing that you might find yourself feeling overwhelmed at tackling. The internet has made gathering information about previously unknown subjects extremely easy, and in an afternoon of study you could learn loads about cooking in an RV, how to downsize from a house, and popular destinations to visit once you're on the road.

Maybe you're more worried about what to do in the worst case scenario, such as if an accident or illness were to occur. Remember my advice from section 3A on setting some of your initial savings aside as an emergency fund; these are the kind of situations that money is meant for.

Or perhaps it's the thought of having to make the big decisions about how much to work, and how far to travel on your own. If you've mostly gone with the flow before in life, or are used to having friends and family always nearby to bounce these questions off of, this can be challenging to get used to.

You'll discover that the more you handle decisions and problems on your own, the more self-reliant you'll become. In some ways I think this might be the most rewarding thing solo RVing teaches a person. In the beginning it will be hard juggling all of the planning and problem solving that getting on the road requires, but the more you do it, the better you'll become.

I bought my RV used from a private seller in Florida, and hauling it back home to South Carolina was the first time I ever hitched up a trailer and towed one in my life. It was terrifying driving it out of Tampa's rush hour traffic that afternoon, but having successfully done that, it could never scare me to that level again. I noticed halfway home that one of my roof rivets was missing, and rain was in the forecast. Panicking wasn't going to do any good, so I picked up a ladder and a roll of duct tape at a Walmart to temporarily solve the problem until I could get home and could look up online to how to replace a rivet. Thus began my education in RV ownership.

Overcoming obstacles like these have improved my self-confidence immensely and made me feel a lot more comfortable about dealing with issues that may crop up on the road. You come to realize that no matter what happens, you have the strength to deal with the problem, and the peace of mind that you get from believing in yourself is so satisfying.

So don't worry too much about having to go it alone. Take it one step at a time and enjoy the feeling of a job well done as each hurdle is jumped. You're going to grow a lot as a person tackling it on your own.

Part 6
Wrapping Up

If you've learned nothing else from this guide, remember that full-time RVing does not have to be deferred until old age. You do not need to wait until retirement, do not need to wait until you're rich, and do not need to wait until you have a partner to go with.

What you will need to do is take a look at your finances, do some inner searching to decide what your needs are for traveling, create a plan for getting on the road, and then put in some hard work.

You now have the tools to make the transition easier, and for added inspiration I invite all of you to stop by interstellarorchard.com and comment or e-mail me with updates on your progress.

Safe travels and happy trails,
Becky

Appendix

Worksheets

The Perfect Small RV Worksheet (from section 2)
A step-by-step process for researching your future home on wheels
Not enough space to write out your answers? Grab a notebook and create your own charts!

1: RV type
First question, motorhome or towable?

	Motorhome	Towable
Pros		
Cons		
My result after weighing options:		

If you decided towable, see the first table below. If motorhome, see the second.

Towables:

Type:	Travel Trailer	TT hybrid	Pop-up	Converted trailer
Pros				
Cons				
My result after weighing options:				

Motorhomes:

Type:	Class C	Class B	Converted van	Truck bed Camper
Pros				
Cons				

My result after weighing options:

2: Getting to specifics
Each question in this section has room to make notes about viability for *your* unique situation as you do research.

Size interested in? There's a tradeoff here – more space, or better maneuvering and gas mileage.

Amenities interested in? How important to you is a shower, oven, gray, black, and fresh water tanks.

Brand interested in? Think about durability for living in, and presence of an online owner's forum.

Floor plan interested in? Think about storage space, and how much room the toilet has for sitting at.

3. Check the price

Now that you've come to a tentative decision, do a search online for that specific RV. Camping World, or a site catered to that brand of RV is a good place to start. If the price range is unreasonable, go back to the above steps and reassess your options until you get to a range that is attainable.

Final price range:

4. The numbers

You need these to know how much weight (i.e. stuff) you can put in your new home. If your RV is going to be a towable, you'll also need them to determine how powerful a tow vehicle you'll need.

GVWR:

Dry weight:

CCC:

The RV Inspection and Question Checklist
(from section 2C)

Questions to Ask in Advance
There's room at the end to add more if needed

Will propane, water, electricity be available to test systems?

Are you willing to show that all appliances are working?

Are you okay with a 3rd party inspection? (if you have the money and want one)

The Checklist – Outside

- Frame, walls, roof (distortion, cracks, corrosion, bubbling – if there are obvious problems, don't buy)
- Caulking (for all rivets, bolts, joints, windows, vents, and everywhere else that a hole has been cut into the frame of the RV – if there are obvious problems, don't buy unless it's a cheap RV and you're willing to fix water damage problems)
- Suspension (springs should have no cracks or inverse curving, rubber should be level side to side with adequate fender clearance)
- General appearance (oxidation, decals, chips, missing paint, dings, trim, etc.)
- Lights (lenses & bulbs for both running lights and porch lights)
- Tires (not only appearance but manufacture dates too, they'll be printed on the tires)
- Outside plumbing& valves (sewer connection, city water connection, fresh water tank inlet and outlet)
- Awning (canvas, crank, support)
- Vents and fans
- Stabilizing jacks
- Windows
- Screens

- Door (fit, seal)
- Spare tire
- Water heater
- Battery condition
- Steps
- TV antenna, cable hookup
- Plumbing hoses and electrical cord (if included)

For towables:
- Emergency Break Away Pin
- Chains
- Tongue jack
- Towing plug (could be 7-pin or 4-pin style, depending on trailer size)

For motorhomes:
- Appearance under hood
- Fluid levels
- Engine noise while running

Inside

- General appearance (smell, cleanliness)
- Upholstery (chairs, cushions, bed)
- Floors (soft spots – if you find any, don't buy unless it's a cheap RV and you can afford to fix water damage)
- Walls (discoloration, water stains – see above)
- Dinette posts (firmness)
- Refrigerator (Gas, 110v AC, and 12v DC modes if applicable)
- Stove
- Stove Hood
- Kitchen sink
- Kitchen plumbing (faucets, drains, visible plumbing)
- Propane heater/furnace
- Water heater
- Water pump
- Cabinets & cabinet door latches
- Windows
- Window blinds

- Toilet
- Shower
- Bathroom sink
- Bathroom plumbing
- Electrical 110v outlets
- Electrical 12v outlet
- Lights
- AC/DC Inverter/converter (test electronics on shore power and off battery)
- Air conditioning
- Closets
- Fire extinguisher
- Vents and fans
- TV (mount, amplifier and cables)
- Screen door

For motorhomes:
- Odometer reading
- Seat belts
- dash gauges

Questions to ask while seeing the RV

About anything on the checklist that seems suspect or missing – Can they verify it works? Will they fix problems before you purchase (get it in writing)?, If they can't fix problems, will they give you a discount?

Will they let you test drive it, if a motorhome?

Tank sizes?

Maintenance records (when where brakes, bearings, refrigerator, engine, etc. last serviced)?

Hitch stuff included, if a towable?

Age of spare tire, if not visible?

Do hoses, hose connectors, power cords come with? (shape they're in)

What about other odds and ends? (Leveling blocks, wheel chocks, water pressure regulator)

Other modifications or optional features? (these may affect the weight)

How long has it been up for sale? (if it's been awhile, ask why)

Owner's manuals included?

The Numbers

The VIN number is (remember to look it up online before buying):

Dry weight:

CCC:

GVWR:

Other Notes
This space is for other comments, questions, and observations, to refer to once you get back home and can think.

The Perfect Tow Vehicle Worksheet (from section 2E)
A step-by-step process for researching your future tow vehicle
Not enough space to write out your answers? Grab a notebook and create your own charts!

1. Calculating the Tow Rating you need

Trailer GVWR x 1.25 =

(Minimum tow rating, with trailer weighing 80% of rating – **your prospective tow vehicle must have at least this for a tow rating!**)

Trailer GVWR x 1.43 =

(Recommended tow rating, with trailer weighing ~ 70% of rating)

2. Tow Vehicle type

	Truck	SUV	Van
Pros			
Cons			
My result after weighing options:			

3. Getting to specifics

This space is for further notes such as desired brand; 2 or 4 door; engine size; tongue weight; seating...

4. Check the price

Now that you've come to a tentative decision, do a search online for that specific vehicle. CarMax or other dealerships with online inventories are a good start. If the price range for both the tow vehicle and RV is unreasonable, go back to the above steps and reassess your options until you get to a range that is attainable.

Final price range for tow vehicle:

Final price range for vehicle + RV:

The Money Worksheet (from section 3)
Calculating how much you need to start full-time RVing, and how to reach that number

Not enough space to write out your answers? Grab a notebook and create your own charts!

How much savings you need

<u>High end of RV (or RV + tow vehicle) price range:</u>
(From previous worksheets)

<u>That number, x 1.5:</u>
(This is your base target number to hit in savings)

<u>Things that may change the base savings number?</u> Think repairs on an older rig, living off of savings, and things in your current house/apartment you will be selling off.

<u>Altered target number:</u>
(Taking the items from the previous question into account)

Cost of Living Will be similar once you're on the road – unless you take deliberate steps to change it.

Month:	1	2	3	Average
Food				
Personal items				
Entertain-ment				
Gas				
Rent/home related				
Re-occurring (phone, insurance, etc.)				
Other				
Total:				

Increasing rate of savings

<u>To cut down my expenses, I am going to:</u>

<u>To bring in more money, I am going to:</u>

Further Study

<u>From 2A:</u> Many small RVers could be described as minimalists to some extent, but for two blogs more specifically focused on minimalism, you can read up on Tammy at www.rowdykittens.com and Tynan at tynan.com/whybeminimalist

<u>From 2B:</u> For more information on the various types of RV, you can find my posts on IO at: www.interstellarorchard.com/2011/12/01/rv-types-explained-motorhomes, and: www.interstellarorchard.com/2011/12/15/rv-types-explained-towables

<u>From 3A and 4A:</u> I wrote an article about downsizing early on at IO when I was in the process of doing it myself, it can be found at: www.interstellarorchard.com/2011/11/21/in-pursuit-of-downsizing

<u>From 3B:</u> Those two blogs for getting out of debt are: www.manvsdebt.com and: www.getrichslowly.com. Both have moved on from the original author to a new crew of writers, but still post good information.

<u>From 3C:</u> The Simple Dollar comes highly recommended from my editor for further help with personal finance. www.thesimpledollar.com

<u>From 3D:</u> Bob over at www.cheaprvliving.com has written extensively about van dwelling, a very inexpensive form of RVing.

<u>From 3E:</u> You can still get out and have a lot of fun as a full-timer on a budget, see: www.interstellarorchard.com/2015/02/20/keeping-entertained-as-a-working-age-full-timer

<u>From 3F:</u> For real world examples of travelers who earn an income online:
- Software developers – Cherie and Chris: www.technomadia.com
- Online educator – Kim: kimbopolo.blogspot.com
- Life coach – Tara: theorganicsister.com (She and her family are living stationary in Florida right now, but full-timed for years on the income she made through her online job)
- Writer – Chris: chrisguillebeau.com
- Musician – Glenn: www.tosimplify.net

- Transcriptionist – Rae: travelswithmiranda.uskeba.ca and www.raecrothers.ca/blog

The three sites I use to find my seasonal work camping jobs:
1. www.coolworks.com
2. www.work-for-rvers-and-campers.com
3. www.workamper.com (This one requires yearly dues, the other two are free)

The two articles I wrote about working at national parks and for Amazon
1. National Parks - www.interstellarorchard.com/2013/04/05/working-at-national-parks-for-rvers
2. Amazon - www.interstellarorchard.com/2012/06/26/about-amazons-camperforce

From 4B: I'm not much of a cook, but several of my blog followers are. You can find more advice about cooking in an RV in the comments section of the blog post I wrote at: www.interstellarorchard.com/2012/05/31/whats-cooking